THE WORLD SOUL

Table of Contents

A Personal Injection

Throughout my life, everytime I hit a roadblock or come to a dead end, I retreat. I don't retreat in the sense that I give up. I retreat to a place of momentary isolation, in an attempt to realign with my values, morals, and to get back on track with God. This started in college. When a relationship would end, or I'd feel lost, I'd go to a wide open field across from our football stadium. This only happened a few times in college. I might have realized that a relationship needed to end, or that maybe I hadn't lost my way, but was just wandering a little off the beaten path. It seemed everytime I did this, the moon would be bright in the night sky and it was with the moon I'd have conversations with. Some would call them "come to Jesus" type of conversations. Maybe they were confessions of a sort? Regardless, it was always the moon there to receive what I had to say. In the moments of silence, answers or conclusions would emerge. These moments would ~~always~~ be valuable resets and I left feeling more focused and realigned.

Recently, I came home one night from work and I was struggling. I had just gone through a break up of a strong, and long lasting relationship. I went outside in the back yard with a cigar and the intention of having one of those reset moments. I needed to clear my mind, get it all out in the air and give all these emotions a platform to speak. When I got settled in, I looked into the night sky, and was disheartened as the moon was completely covered in a vast sky of gray. The moonlight barley filtered out behind the continuous sea of clouds. It was an image of how I felt. I felt lost and covered up like that moon. Determined to get it all out anyway, I smoked my cigar and talked to the ground before me. I spent about an hour talking it out and emptying my inner thoughts, problems, concerns, and dreams out loud. Slowly, my confusion and the knot of emotions that went with it, began to untangle and clear out. I came to an epiphany, and began to laugh. Clarity had set in. I smiled, and looked up to the night sky. I hadn't looked up since starting this inner dialogue. The waves of cloudy sky swam past and there, right as I looked up, the moon became visible in it's nest of stars and the clouds shifted as I stared up in my moment of clarity. Bright as could be, full with white light, the moon floated in the parting of the clouds. At the moment of my reaching clarity, it seemed the sky had reached some clarity too.

I thought for a moment: Maybe the world really does reflect us in some way. Maybe we are connected, us and this world, by some unseen bridge.

Chapter One:
The Stirrings of Gaia

Something has changed. Something IS changing. Something is different. That something is our world. It's changing so much. Most people living through this time in history would likely say the world is changing everyday. Politics, Religion-based issues, Education, Income, Hourly Wage Rates, Television, Film, Wi-fi, our phones...all are in a constant state of flux; constant evolution.

Carl Jung said, "No one can know the greater good for all"[1], but anyone can recognize when something is beginning to sink. There is something seemingly getting worse. A type of darkness swiftly moves to overtake us.

Depression. Anxiety. Drowning lonliness... suicide. These are invisible, ghostly spectres that fly to blanket us when we are our most vulnerable. These are entities that appear to be multiplying and spreading. Frequently more people seem to be plagued by them. Evermore I find myself and others searching like a lighthouse over dark choppy waters of the night. The ship we sought; submerged. That ship's name: "Meaning". Or was it "Purpose"? I can't recall.

Why are we here? How'd we get lost?

How did we become so concrete? That is what we are becoming is it not? Chronic back pain ails us. Neck strains seem part of the job description for most corporate jobs. Rigid, tight, immobilized, stiff backs, stiff shoulders...stiff hearts; the chiropractors can only fix so much. We become heavier and heavier, more dense, more 'real', more literal. A transformation into concrete gargoyles. Most times, laying in bed all day is the most enticing choice.

The world in flux around us rushes by, while most of us sink in the quicksand. Our heavy hearts are too much of an anchor. Our heavy souls have too much weight. There's the word I was looking for; SOUL. Our souls are heavy. Spirit, soul, anima... energy. Whatever you must call it. It's solidifying.

I think this abjectivity is a direct consequence of the solidifying of the soul of the world. The world has a soul? What do I mean by that? The world has a soul and we've neglected it. Ignored it, rationalized it away. And then we gasp, gawk, and shout in utter appall at the fact that most people do not care about environmental protective action. Save and revivify the world soul; you will get an environmental movement. But you will not achieve that through fear mongering. Not through catastrophizing. Yet unfortunately that is mostly what the environmental movements do now: catastrophize. The figureheads of this movement always string together rhetoric that is alarming, and fear inducing. Impending doom hangs over our heads. That's been the bird song of environmentalists for over thirty years now.

I'm not a climate denier let me state it clearly now. There are horrible things we're intentionally doing to the oceans and the environment that can, and need to be prevented. But the talk of the climate activists is dangerous. I see more and more people losing their minds over these issues. This leads to a fever of passion by the movement's members that usually result in rigid, dogmatic and exoteric stances that try to aggressively batter those not completely agreeing, into submissive compassion for the planet. It ends up pushing more people away. I believe it's the wrong approach, and that the true solution could be found in a reestablishing, and reimagining of the world soul, that in turn could possibly strengthen our own souls.

Save the world soul, and maybe save yours…

With Facebook, Instagram, Twitter, and the normal news networks, it feels as if not a day goes by without hearing about environmentalist action. Climate change activism has even infiltrated our shows and movies. Art and entertainment has always been a platform for political beliefs and ideologies. Yet there is seemingly a shift in the tempo and pace of the climate activism of today. It seems to be getting more catastrophic. Suddenly now, climate change and the end of the world go hand in hand, most often they are in the same sentence together. Representative Alexandria Ocasio-Cortez told people in 2019 that we only had 12 years to live. TO LIVE. Rising star of the environmentalist movement, Greta Thunberg preaches similar consequences. Most of the time she's preaching about how climate change has already catastrophically altered *her* life. If you look at the headlines or news feeds, the short hand is always something frighteningly world shattering. I can understand why one would use this method in an attempt to jar people out of their inactive slumber.

But this has been the tone for some thirty years now if not more. Let us go back to 1975 when the cover of "Science News" magazine had New York City completely covered in ice, clamoring that the next ice age was on the way.[2] More recently we could remember the claim that Siberia and Europe were going to be twins after the coming world wide freeze, a claim made in 2007![3] There was also "Science Digest" in 1975 saying we didn't have the comfortability of distance before the next ice age.[4] In fact, global temperatures were beginning to fall around 1940, leading scientists in 1970 to speculate we were heading towards a new ice age.[5] Research of that time held that from 1880 to 1950 was the hottest the Earth had ever been.[6] This fed into the fear mongering of the coming ice age. Of course science improves as we become smarter and our technology advances; I understand that. I don't have a problem with the long history of the back and forth outcomes of the ice age, or the warming that has occupied the climate activist/environmentalist movements for nearly the past 100 years. My concern is with how these messages were delivered. Because just as our technology advances and we become smarter, so too does our effectiveness to sell a frightening headline, and create as much fear as possible to get the biggest reaction we can. Climate Scientist Mike Hulme said:

"Yes, climate change is real and humans are definitely partly responsible for it. But words like 'catastrophic', phrases such as 'climate change is worse than we thought,' and claims that we are approaching 'irreversible tipping in the earth's climate' and are 'at the point of no return' are simply used as unguided weapons with which forlornly to threaten society into behavioral change."[7]

If I haven't lost you already, I'd like to make sure to reemphasize what has already been said twice above so far: our negative effect on the climate is real. There are indeed horrible acts we commit against our Earth. But as Hulme also says, "The language of catastrophe is not the language of Science."[8] So then what is it the language of? I've come to the conclusion that it sounds more like the language of religion, like the language of faith. After all, most of the figure heads of climate change have proposed plans that are so outrageously drastic, that they are quite literally asking for your faith in the belief that they know what is best, and that their answer is THE answer. Solutions like Ocasio-Cortez's "Green New Deal", which calls for radical changes in many facets of human life, like restructuring all of America's infrastructure by replacing all buildings with eco friendly material, are part and parcel to the typical political solution to a problem. If it isn't large, massive and expensive answers as such, then the go to is always hardcore carbon emission cuts, usually done in the most expensive and creative ways. But as research shows, for political and economic reasons, tough carbon cuts are not the way to go as there are smarter and more efficient answers.[9] It is very easy for politicians, activists, and idealists to get carried away by lavish technological hypotheses on how to save the planet. But the truth of the matter is that most of them will not be ready in terms of scalability or stability.[10] That is the massive pitfall of most of Cortez's "Green New Deal". The money needed for such drastic technological changes would perhaps be better spent on basic research and development in most areas. That is really one of the biggest knots in the whole situation. Climate activists and scientists would rather invest in alarmism, instead of investing in smart solutions or research for smart work arounds.

Solutions such as the ocean plastic cleanup suggested by the young dutch inventor Boyan Slat. Unfortunately, it may just be easier to stoke the fire of fear and despair. But we must think of the dangers of such an attitude. There's the chance to fall right into a positive feedback loop. Activists must scare the public into caring. Some of the public cares as an answer but not enough. Activists or politicians up the ante and the consequences are much more severe, much more near. More people care, but others continue on about their day. Then one side ups the ante a little more. And then a little more. All the while, nothing detrimental is really changing. So for the most part, a vast majority of people are becoming desensitized to the back and forth of the climate catastrophe talk. That's one of the gravest dangers and an unspoken consequence of this whole movement. The stakes are rising higher and higher as the fight to get more people to care ensues. I believe this has caused some to go to extreme measures. Between politicians and voices of the movement claiming we only have a few years to live, or even some scientists publishing work that hasn't been peer reviewed[11], the ends begin to justify the means. In ways, that is more of a danger to me than climate change, especially when it is a method being used by people in positions of power.

Underneath these surface level movements, I see a subsurface current beginning to take wind in its sails. Underneath the science, politics, and activism, I see a growth in the spiritual, religious side of this movement. All the fear mongering speeches before the UN or at award shows was beginning to remind me of those fire and brimstone Baptist preachers of old that we all know too well. This type of preacher is almost an archetype in the American psyche now, but also still real, still personified in parts of the country. The over zealous, devout believer that wants to convert as many blind gentiles as he or she can before the coming of the end times; sounds to me like a climate activist today. In our current mode, the positive feedback loop of alarmism has forced environmentalism to become rigid with fundamentalism. Fundamentalism meaning, "My way is the right way, and the only way." A trap so often met in religions, fundamentalism, can infiltrate ideologies too. It has infiltrated the environmentalist ideology. This fundamentalism has even seeped into the science of environmental issues. Dissenters who dare attempt to publish data that goes against the alarmism, see their research defunded, their reputations slandered, and their work buried as said so by climate scientist Richard Lindzen from MIT.[12] As fundamentalism begins to set in on this movement, it's figure heads become more impassioned, the alarmism grows, and we start to see what could be the unspoken and unlabeled movements of quasi-religious activism. There seems to be some causal connection with fundamentalism and the soul.

"Perhaps we can think of fundamentalism as a stifling, asphyxiation, and constipation of the soul." - Tom Cheetham[13]

It leaves no surprise in me then when I come to this realization that the environmentalist movement is becoming religious. It seems the inevitable conclusion. There exists a group of faithful believers who are becoming more frustrated at those people and systems who continue to show a dangerous lack of regard for the environment around them. Naturally, fanaticism and extremism will rise:

"Fanaticism and extremism are our own impulsive and compulsive angers and passions raised to a higher pitch and given an architecture rendering them more coherent and more systematic. Then they seem not merely the urges of private inner demons, but wear a public face that can be displayed and marketed to an audience." - Tom Cheetham[14]

If, as I am suggesting, the movement is becoming fundamentally religious, then who is their god?

I cannot help but look at our current situation with the climate and the purveyors of radical climate change and not see undertones of the soul and psyche. The movement itself is the very architecture mentioned above that gives a coherent system to the compulsive angers and passions raised to a higher pitch. The environmentalists movement has indeed become the vehicle for such passions. A vehicle that will not stop and does not seem to care how many people it labels as 'unbelievers' get run over along it's war path.

I see these as symptoms. Symptoms of a sick soul. It is there that I would turn for solutions. Not alarmist headlines. Not politicians. Not child activists. Not picket signs and blockading streets with my protest. The soul. My soul, and the world's soul. I find myself not thinking the climate movement has gone completely wrong in their moving closer to religious fervor. It is indeed something spiritual that is the problem. But I think the more I research this issue, I realize they aren't going deep enough. They are still caught up in the material surface level, clinging desperately to life and a hope for a future. Down in the muck and dirt of the deepest parts of the soul is where the truth lay. Alchemists of old had a saying, "In the filth it will be found." A claim understood to mean that, what it was you were looking for, would most likely be found where you least wanted to look. Yet, the whole of Alchemy, the precursor to natural science, had an aim to discover the spiritual side of matter and the material world. Alchemy wasn't a crazed half animal first attempt at science. The early alchemists were philosophers of the truest since, seeking wisdom and specifically; wisdom of the soul. They believed the remnants of god filled the natural world and could be experimentally experienced. They also believed their external work was an exact mirror of the work being done on themselves internally. Their work on the world was also work on their souls. They tried to find the world's soul while finding theirs. In ways I think that is also what that statement meant. In the filth of the material world, there can be found soul. Regardless, the issue is internal. That is where true life and a true future reside. But if this is not realized, then dangerously the religion of environmentalism will continue to grow and solidify. I've heard it said that we all have a God-shaped hole in our hearts, and man will find whatever he can to fill that hole. The radical climate activists have begun to fill that hole with the Earth. They fill that god shaped hole not with a god, but with a goddess. Slowly they are reawakening the dark mother, Gaia, from her slumbers. Our culture is increasingly materialistic, and our rampant materialism is a large part of the issues we are here discussing. I bring this up because the etymology of material or matter derives from "Mater" or mother. There is some type of hidden connection in our materialism and the reawakening of the Mother Earth archetype. They are beginning to send her prayers and offerings, in hopes that they can save her. They will resurrect her bones into colossal status and pray that she brings her wrath upon those capitalists, deniers, or any who defile her body. Already they see Gaia's hand behind the hurricanes, tornadoes, tsunamis and earthquakes. These are her stirrings as she climbs from the shadowy abyss. They know not what they resurrect. Gaia, Mother Earth, does not discern between the faithful and the deniers when she is hungry. She only devours. Nature is amoral. The lion that kills the gazelle does not do so because she's a bad lion, and likes to murder. And the gazelle is not a hapless innocent. There are indeed no morals out in nature. Richard Dawkings taught us so with his "Selfish Gene". Even what appears to be altruism in animals is mere instinct. There is no dying for the good of others, or making the 'right' choice. Just instinct. Well Nature's and Gaia's instinct is bloody. Mother Earth has no moral hierarchy. There is growth, and there is decay. In Gaia's kingdom, there is the constant birthing of life, and the continual screams of death.

"Nature rejoices in nature; nature subdues nature; nature rules over nature." - Democritus

If you'd like to resurrect this goddess because of your inner angers and passions bubbling to the brim, bringing about fanaticism and extremism, then go ahead. But this is not a solution if your true aim is to stop climate change and save the world. This is a solution if your aim is to scare as many people as you can into buying into what you believe is right. Or this may be your solution if you are possessed by an apocalyptic obsession. Something I'll explore later.

******

To save the world from catastrophic climate change, we must look inward into our souls, and that of the world's soul. We get so caught up on the surface or on the material. Ever since the enlightenment, we've felt that the material was the only empirical truth and therefore all our battles have been, and continue to be, fought there. But that is not where the battle for the world soul, and the salvation of the Earth must be fought. The deeper levels of noosphere (think consciousness, rationality, interpersonal relationships) and the soul are where the answers are. Nooshpere being another word for the deepest interiors of our mind, or of our psyche. This deep interior is where the battle really resides:

"Gaia's main problems are not industrialization, ozone depletion, overpopulation, or resource depletion. Gaia's main problem is the lack of mutual understanding and mutual agreement in the noosphere about how to proceed with those problems. We cannot rein in industry if we cannot reach mutual understanding and mutual agreement based on a world centric moral perspective concerning the global commons. And we reach the world centric moral perspective through a difficult and laborious process of interior growth and transcendence... global problems demand global consciousness, and global consciousness is the product of five or six major stages of development." - Ken Wilber[15]

The noosphere and the deeper, more internal levels of consciousness and humanity are where we must turn. Because not everybody is born wanting to take care of the Earth. That state of consciousness requires a global perspective. It requires a state of being that allows exiting the simply personal perspective. A perspective like that requires a transcending of the ego. The ego being that identity which we think is really us. The ego is that rider who holds the reigns of your mind during the workings of the day. Or so we think. More on that later. Regardless, to move past the ego is something near impossible when most of us are not even aware there is more to the ego, and most of us are only looking externally for answers. Not everyone is ready for such a task as being able to have a global perspective that would see caring for the earth as an option. Our advances in psychology have shown that there are different temperaments to personality and with those tempera-ments comes different leanings towards moral standards. Moral psychologist Johnathan Haidt has done a lot in these regards. In a way, your personality tendencies determine what it is you care about morally. There isn't just a cut and dry good and bad. Some people care about cleanliness and order more than the person who cares about empathy and equality. Beyond all that is the perspective of a global consciousness. To be conscious of you, your actions, and how they pertain to the state, nation, country, and world, requires some great developments internally. It requires you moving beyond the ego. Not everyone is there yet, and to stomp around yelling and condemning those who aren't caring about the global environment enough, is actually pushing more people away. See, what we are actually discussing is internal or what Ken Wilber would call, "Left Hand" issues. "Left Hand" because they fall onto the left side of his Integral Psychology graph. Really, the left side of these graphs just refers to everything unseen, and everything internal. Contrary to that is the right hand side and that is where all the external factors of reality reside. An example of this would be the Brain, which is a material, factual and empirical subject we can study and has indeed been studied much. It can be cut into and operated on. It is therefore a right side or external factor. It's opposite would be Mind...something a little less concrete but no less empirical. Some of the greatest neurosurgeons have had to come to the conclusion, most often at the end of their careers, that despite how much research they did, there was always a division between mind and brain.

It is in the problem of this dichotomy of right and left hand that the climate change movement has been caught up in. It wants global change, which can only be found in the left hand internal side of things, while continuing forward with attempts only on the right hand external side:

"...very few can actually take a world centric or postconventional perspective. But if the entire Left Hand is ignored and devalued - if we ignore interiors and just rivet our eyes on a Right Hand 'global' map of Gaia or systems nature - we will ignore the actual path of getting people to that global or world centric stance. We will have a goal with no path." - Ken Wilber[16]

Well how do we get everyone to reach a global consciousness? How can you get people to begin to step outside of the purely subjective and perhaps start to see things from not only other people's viewpoints but from the viewpoint of the world?

What if I told you that this type of worldview used to be natural to us as humans? What if I told you, ancient man didn't see such a stark division between subjective and objective in the world around him? I think the next logical question would be; then where did it all go wrong? Or, how do we get it back?

First: what is it we lost?

Chapter Two

What We Have Lost

James Hillman said, "Wherever the language of psychopathology (crisis, breakdown, collapse) occurs, the psyche is speaking of itself in pathologized terms, attesting to itself as subject of the pathos."[17] We are currently surrounded by the language of psychopathology. Indeed that is primarily the only type of language used by the environmental movement. If we are to believe Hillman, and the countless others who have said similar things, then we are indeed suffering as a people from psychic issues. This is just a symptom though. The heart of the matter is yet to be revealed and I intend for us to find it together now. I think a starting point would be to find the origins of our current worldview. Above, when I mentioned things like soul, or psyche, or undercurrents of religious fervor, I immediately felt a pang of hesitation. A little voice tried convincing me that using such terms or taking this essay down that way will lead to no avail. People don't want to hear about all that, because all of that is mumbo-jumbo-woo! It is not empirical science. It is not data. It is not cold hard facts. But this view on such things is not my own, because when I try to live the rationalistic and materialistic worldview out, I find many shortcomings. In fact this world view isn't everybody's natural perspective, it is inherited from an era of thinkers and hypotheses that drastically changed not only our minds but also our perspectives on nature, and our collective place in the world. I'm talking about the revolutionary thought handed down to us by the likes of Descartes, Copernicus, Newton, and the many more facets of the Scientific Revolution, and the Enlightenment. See, it is ever since these moments in time that human-kind has declared we now have a cap on reality via the empiricism of science. Underneath this cap, everything we can explain scientifically and rationalistically. Above it; things we cannot explain, and are therefore less real and worse; not even noteworthy. The problem with such an inherited world view is that this leaves out many things but primarily concepts like meaning, value, purpose; these are things that do not have an equation to prove its existence or data to track it's movements. Of the aforementioned names, I think Copernicus might be the most unwittingly conspirator of this inherited materialist worldview. It was he after all that really pushed the radical shift from a view of the cosmos where the earth was the center, to a cosmos of the Sun as the center of our solar system. Indeed this is the more scientifically accurate world view and I'm not going to slide into the realm of saying we need to revert back to an Earth centered perspective or the regions of flat earthers. Yet the unspoken consequences of such a transition were this: over time, with the aid of science, we came to realize that Copernicus was right and that unfortunately that meant we were just a giant space rock floating through the endless vacuum of space around a sun that would eventually eat us alive and oh by the way, we're one of trillions and trillions of such bodies of floating rock in an ever expanding universe. With such a cold, distant, and isolating cosmos as our perspective, is it any wonder why people now look at the night sky full of stars and instantly feel a wave of anxiety and littleness towards the infinite? In one swift move, The Enlightenment and Scientific Revolution made Human-kind to feel like an accident, living in a world of dead objective things that can all be explained away with time and inspection.

With the aid of Descartes, it soon came to pass that the only thing that really mattered was the human intellect. "I think therefore I am"... that was the only thing Descartes could prove to be real in an objective world of science. From then on everything had to fit into that lens, the lens of human rational thinking, or else it wasn't real. Again, this left the whole "left hand" side of reality out. The transcendental, the internal, psychic, mind-related, soul-related, spiritual and purposeful side of reality was cast aside. No more could there be wonder or intrigue in the world around us. Eventually it would all be given a name, a class, a species, and then written down in books and that was that. No more mystery, no more fantasy, no more soul:

"Their notions (cartesians, scientific materialists) abetted the murder of the World's Soul by cutting apart the hearts natural activity into sensing facts on one side and intuiting fantasties on the other, leaving us images without bodies and bodies without images, an immaterial subjective imagination. Severed from an extended world of dead objective facts...to sense penetratingly we must imagine, and to imagine accurately we must sense." - James Hillman[18]

I disagree with Hillman when he says the World's soul has been murdered. It is still out there. I don't think the likes of us could murder such a force. But we can dangerously neglect it to the point of catastrophe. Us moderns seem to have lost all sense. We are lost and we can't even imagine solutions for the problems that face us. On top of that, anxiety and depression run rampant. Our place in this world seems lost. What purpose is there to life? What is the meaning of all this? The suffering, cruelty, and the isolation all seep down into our bones. There is no answer out there, and inwards? How am I supposed to navigate that? What is my meaning? What is my purpose here? The world around you churns and grinds on it's ever twisting gears and moves at breakneck pace. It has no time to stop for you and worry about if you're getting along or not.

"A world without souls offers no intimacy. Things are left out in the cold, each object by definition cast away even before it is manufactured, lifeless litter and junk, taking its value wholly from consumptive desire to have and to hold, wholly dependent on the subject to breathe it into life with personal desire. When particulars have no essential virtue, then my own virtue as a particular depends wholly and only on my subjectivity or on your desire for me, or fear of me: I must be desirable, attractive, a sex object, or win importance and power." - James Hillman[19]

My proposed answer to the problem of climate change and it's radical shifting towards a quasi-religious, fundamentalist movement, is for us not to catastrophize about our impending doom, but to turn inward. Yet in our world today, we are solely focused on the external. Despite the fact, as stated above, that internal diseases like depression and suicide run rampant in our culture, we don't seem to know where to turn. These illnesses, these specters that haunt us hold the clue in their very make up. Their origin is beyond external material. They come from the internal, psychic realm. And we can't enter that threshold from a merely empirically led scientific stance. That key won't unlock that door, it won't even fit. I am finding that we desperately must become aware of the fact that our conscious egos that we think make up our internal psyche are just part of the picture. What do I mean by the conscious ego? I mean that which you think is you. That which you think is your thinking brain. I mean that which is behind your eyes reading this. I mean that which is behind your ears receiving and processing what it hears. That processing computer behind your forehead is your conscious ego driven mind. But that is only part of the picture. That is merely a little paddle boat, lost at sea. And the sea is raging. That sea is the unconscious element of our mind. Depth psychology for decades since Freud has done much to explore the boundaries of this unconscious realm. But one thing that has been shown time and time again is that it is actually this part of your brain, that does most of the button pushing when it comes to you and how you act. Now this is a doubly important factor: (1) because the more unaware we are of the unconscious influences that pressure our actions, then the more you and I will continue to behave in ways we end up wishing we hadn't. We will continue to have all the best intentions, and still find a way to mess things up, or say the wrong thing. Maybe you don't believe me. Maybe you're asking how it could be that the you that you think is you, is actually only part of the picture. I know this is so though because I continue daily, to fail at controlling myself. I can't fully control my emotions, my fantasies, my actions sometimes. All because there are factors beyond my conscious mind that need my attention and need to be integrated. A prime example of this is anger. Sometimes we become possessed by anger and do things we really regret. We'll start that fight, or say those words we can never take back. I used the word 'possessed' because that is literally what these unconscious motivations will do; they'll possess you! As long as we are blind to the unconscious and its inhabitants, (because it is deeply inhabited, packed full like sardines in there) then we will continue to shadow project onto our enemies, and we will continue to put not only our lives, but the lives of the whole world in danger. Our technology has advanced in a way that around the world, people hover with their hands over buttons that with one push, could completely annihilate the whole planet. We live too far away from the Cold War, and have forgotten the necessary seriousness that war brought with it. The fate of the world hangs in the balance of individual humans. How are their minds? How is the mental state of those individuals? Are they aware that sometimes, it isn't them having emotions, but their emotions having them? What happens when one of them loses control? It only takes one, one individual, to lose control of their psychic standing and the rest is lost history.

The unconscious is also important because, (2) to use the imagery of the paddle boat at sea; that sea of your unconscious, is actually just a drop, in the ancient, massive, crashing and raging ocean that is the collective unconscious. Now much has been debated about where this sea hits shore and I'm not sure one can ever fully know. But what we can know is that Ancient man was a little more unconscious than us. What I mean by that is their conscious egos were still developing in a way. They had easier access to the unconscious and the collective unconscious. They interacted with the archetypal personalities that populate the unconscious regularly. We can see so in the symbols and images that have been created through history. Ancient man didn't take things so literal. There was still metaphor. There were still symbols. Things were numinous, meaning they had layers and depths that weren't just shallow definitions. Ancient Humans also found soul in the world around them. The world was so ensouled, that there were gods almost everywhere. In the forest were found nymphs. In the oceans, mermaids and sirens who could pull sailors off course. The wind carried voices. The sun was a life giving father. The earth a sacrificial mother who tore herself asunder so that new life could be reborn. These weren't the adolescent wonderings of pre scientific Neanderthals. This was a vision of the world with a soul. This was a perspective that still understood there was more to the world and more to man than just what the conscious ego driven eyes saw before them. Just because our ancient ancestors didn't have science, does not mean that they were less sophisticated than us. Our progressive mindsets love to look at history as if it's been a straight line leaning upwards every year from zero to present, with the present at the highest on the charts because we're so "advanced". Ancient man was profound in their thinking and we know this because much studying of our early myths has been done. Myth didn't mean fake or made up. The Ancient Greek the word myth came from was 'musterion' which meant more something akin to believing without seeing, or in other words; faith. It was a form of religion and then some. Joseph Campbell studied a multitude of myths around the world, originating from different people of different times. He found that all these myths essentially tell the same storied foundation and Campbell equates this world wide, time crossing coincidence, as relating back to the psyche. The myths studied came from different genders, races, cultures, gods but the human psyche was the only common element in all of those myths around the world. Psychologically, ancient humans used myth as vessels containing the instruction on how to act and passed these stories down to their generations to come. Myths were the stories that ancestors fed with their souls, and used to feed and guide the souls of their youth. When looked at from this lens, myths are profound. Myths are reflections of the colorful vastness of our souls.

Yet today, the human of modernity hardly bothers with this whole world inside them, lying in the deep. This is to our continuing detriment. Depth psychology has also shown that when these unconscious energies are not given conscious attention, when they are not dialogued with or acknowledged, they don't just go away. They become repressed or suppressed. Suppression and repression are different. Suppression of unconscious factors takes more energy and usually daily. In the unconscious there are darker realities to who you are, one being the shadow. The shadow is the personality bundled with all the darker thoughts, desires, hatreds, resentments, and fantasies of yours that you'd rather not let see the light of day. Those things don't go away, the shadow doesn't just disappear. They bubble up to the surface and some people actively fight to suppress them. Modern religion has aided in the process as it so often tells you to fight and suppress those evil desires of the shadow and then misidentifies them with some external factor like original sin or the devil, but never you. Repression takes less energy but is just as dangerous. Repressed are those unconscious elements you've forgotten or ignored. Again, they don't go away. None of this goes away. The shadow and other unconscious elements want to be heard and will eventually fight to the surface of day and that is usually through projections. We project onto others our own shadows, our own unconscious content. This projection leaves us vulnerable to then also being possessed by unconscious content. I think this is what is happening today in the environ-mentalist movements.

We as moderns have continually neglected the darker, unconscious realm of our psyche, and because of that, we are dangerously ignorant. We're not only dangerously ignorant to our own devil within, but also dangerously ignorant to those archetypal personalities that people the unconscious and possess us. This is what I mean when I say that I think these climate movements are resurrecting Gaia, or Mother Earth. The great terrible mother is an archetypal personality. It shows up continually in myth and fairy tale all throughout human history. It's a psychological characteristic that sometimes finds reality in the evil step mother of ours, or the mother we had that was too hard, too driven by discipline, and didn't show enough care. This very real archetypal personality is breaking through the surface of the ocean and I think possessing much of those maddened and enraged acolytes of the environmentalist movement. One of the central themes of Jung's teachings, was that people don't have ideas, ideas have people. Could not our failing to be aware of the perspective that ancient man had pre-enlightenment, pre-conscious driven egoism, have gotten us into a place where we are possessed by a movement of instinctual emotion that burns with passion? Could not our failing to be aware of the unconscious have dangerously placed us in a state of neglect for the Soul of the world and our soul as well?

There is a line drawn in the sand of the beach that is history. That line is the threshold we crossed without knowing. The doorway we entered blindly. The crossing of the Enlightenment. The crossing of the Scientific Revolution. Those pivotal centuries: the 11th and 12th centuries, saw us off in a new direction. The rational mind was king now. Spirits, soul, the imaginary, fantasy, astrology, and others of their kind had no place in this new world. Human-kind set out to understand nature to its fullest capacity, in what now seems to be an unconscious attempt to control it. That is exactly the next logical step after picking nature apart. Once we realized we could objectify the world around us, bring nature down to merely an "it", or an objective "what", then we could learn how to manipulate it. This has been the unspoken aim of the scientific enlightenment since it's emergence. With the objectification of the world down to merely matter, mass, fauna, atoms, molecules, and the likes, came the objectification of Human-kind. The world around us broke down into severed pieces with no life that could be thrown into the lab and observed in an attempt to control. To know is to control. Mankind sets out to know every last corner of the world around it, and then tries to manipulate it all in a show of our superiority. Meanwhile, perhaps from unconscious drives, Mankind's last conquest of nature will be its conquest of itself. All this because the soul was ripped out of it all. All of this because we stumble blind dangerously into the future, because we are unaware of what really controls us.

This isn't just about environmentalism or catastrophizing global warming. As I've written this book and read and learned along the way, I'm starting to realize that this is just one more symptom, of a larger, far more engrossing sickness. I write this now, in the middle of a nation wide quarantine during the breakout of the coronavirus. The whole world is in a pandemic. The whole world has come to a screeching stop because of a disease. I can't help but believe that this disease, originated in nature, is an external reflection of our internal sickness globally. I can't help but think that the external virus is just a symptom of the true disease in all of our minds. How do we move forward?

Chapter Three

What Do We Do?

It seems the issue of environmentalism becoming an extremist religious movement, is tied together with our self inflicted mental dis-ease. Since the scientific revolution and egoistic Cartesian renaissance, we have neglected not only the deeper realms of our psyche, but the psyche of the world. Psyche comes from the Greek word meaning Soul. In fact, it is words that are essential to one of the two propositions for practical solutions that I will explore. For if the issue is self inflicted, then there is good news. This means that we can by chance find self discovered solutions.

I'm trying to approach this issue practically. When I really think about it I try to break it down to basics: what is it that we can actually control. I mean you and I, individuals like ourselves. What is it that we could do? Odds are you and I have little influential power over the world to make great change. But to me, in ways that is not wholly true. The collection of all humanity is made of a bunch of different individuals. If the unconscious aspects of our psyche are indeed collective, or connected to every other individual with a collective consciousness out there, then we are connected to the whole collective in a unique way. In other words, we are each individually connected to the collective of humanity in a special way. In some ways that I'm still trying to grapple with, you and I as individuals, are responsible for the actions of the collective. I know this is true in at least the way that the atrocities of humankind were done by HUMANS. The makeup of those humans of the past is the exact same make up in you. The evil in their bones rests in yours. Regardless, this puts a special responsibility on us as individuals. When it comes to responsibility, what is it that we have direct control over? Depth psychology has shown that often we are controlled by unconscious factors. It's a whole other book and experiment to figure out how to solve that issue. But when it comes to the here and now, you and I have control over some things. We can at least put up a conscious effort towards having a certain perspective of the world, and using certain words. Those are in fact my two propositions for how we could possibly move forward in light of the conclusions come to in this book. Words, and perspective.

Why words? Speech is important. What you say about yourself and others can become reality. It was indeed with spoken word that God is attributed with creating most of reality, in the collected origin myths of religions around the world. If we are indeed made in his image, then our ability to use words and speech are reflective of our potential capacity to create order out of the chaos that is reality. What could words have to do with our soul, and the soul of the world? Since the cataclysmic shift in our history from a world of pre science, to one seeping with rationalistic materialism due to the birth of science, there has been a shift in our language. Not only a shift in our language, but also how we use language as a way to interpret the world around us. We have become very literal. In ways, we have become impatient with language. We don't have time for things to be numerous in their definitions or meanings. We have sanitized language down to a literal, point-blank interpretation, and consequently, done the same to the world around us. Depth psychologist James Hillman has this example:

"'How was the bus ride?" I respond, "miserable, terrible, desperate." But these words describe ME, my feelings, my experience, not the bus ride which was bumpy, crowded, steamy, cramped, noxious, with long waits. Even if I noticed the bus and the trip my language transferred the attention to notions about myself. The "I" has swallowed the bus, and my knowledge of the external world has become a subjective report of my feelings." [20]

This is a great example of how our language steals the soul right out from the depths of the world around us. We are constantly speaking in a subjective way that leads us to the illusion that we are saying something about something else, but we are really usually only describing ourselves. Ever since the enlightenment and the scientific revolution our use of adjectives and descriptive language, have moved from describing the environment around us, to describing ourselves. We have culturally lost or are lacking a sense of poetic speech. In our industrial economy, there's just no time for descriptive words. Tell me what it is now. Even typing that felt arrogant. Arrogant because we think we can cover the whole basis of what a thing is, with one word. We label and we conceptualize. Social media has made things worse, broken language down, disintegrated it into fractured pieces. Newspaper headlines must be shorter, louder, more bombastic; there's no time for truth. Tweets must be harsh, dark, and rude if you want to go viral. Reading a book is frowned upon more than ever. I think every generation since the 1900's has had that same complaint but I can't help but think it's especially worse now with technology. Our attention spans are shrinking rapidly. On Instagram or Snapchat, there is the option to post a "story"...as if you can fit a whole person's story inside of fifteen to thirty seconds. I think there is power in our language, and we need to pay very close attention to not only how we speak about ourselves, but to how we speak about the world around us. Such attention would be like harkening back to an old idea known as "Notitia". Hillman describes it:

"Attention to the qualities of things resurrects the old idea of notitia as a primary activity of the soul. Notitia refers to that capacity to form true notions of things from attentive noticing." [21]

Attentive noticing. Careful attention to our speech. Vigilant awareness of how we speak and the words coming out of our mouths. One of the symptoms of our soul sickness I see is a growing lack of found meaning, and value in the world. People are continually looking around trying to figure out where they fit into the picture, and how they can find meaning in this life they've been handed. There are people out there looking for value. I think we won't find it again until we start to use language that is infused with value and virtue. That's what James Hillman calls us to use: Language of value and virtue.[22] Start using adjectives and descriptive words that give value to the world around you.

"This respect demands reconstitution of our language so that it speaks again of *qualities* -- naming what is there, rather than what we **feel** about what is there and abstraction away from what is there." [23]

In today's time I think we're beginning to shy away from language of values and virtues because we're afraid to value certain things over others.

When you say you value something, or instill it with words of value, you automatically create a hierarchy. With the political agendas infused in today's language, we can't dare value too much and create a hierarchy that might hurt someone's feelings and displace them in a position less than someone else. If we want to find a soul again in the world around us, which ultimately leads to more people caring about this planet we're on, then we must get back to using descriptive words. Words that describe color, texture, and size. Words of virtue like right, wrong, good, beautiful, and true.

But, and this leads me to my next proposition of practical solutions, this notitia also refers to careful attention to the cosmos.

I don't necessarily mean "cosmos" in the way that we know it, meaning space. The old Greek "Kosmos" originally meant something more akin to cosmetology, or more specifically, aesticis. The cosmos of reality was a reality of cosmetic design. To ancient man, man before scientific enlightenment, everything was beautiful. Ancient Humans, when they created, took great care to make sure there was beauty manifested in the creation. From totem masks of tribes, to ancient cave drawings, to Greek architecture, to Middle Ages gothic cathedrals, humans tried to make the world around them aesthetically pleasing, and in consequence, ensouled the world. In contrast to today, what comparison do we have? Things around us are mass produced.

There seems to be a prioritizing of conformity in design, and a lack of uniqueness.

"Psychotherapy needs to affirm the sufferings of the heart, is dis-ease in the world of things, that they are ugly empty, wrong, bereft of a sensemaking cosmos, and by this affirmation that yes we are heart-sick because we are thing-sick, psychotherapy will lift the an-esthetized stupor from our reactions, lift the repression in the ugliness of things themselves, so that psychotherapy can move again, in the direction that the symptoms are leading it, now toward an appreciation of the world ensouled." [24]

We are "Thing-sick". With a careful attention to our words about ourselves, and the world around us, and with careful attention to beautifying the reality (cosmos) around us, we can perhaps find a cure. It might not be a great example, but here's a personal anecdote to this idea. My grandpa has always beautified his backyard in whichever house he lives in. In my lifetime he has only lived in two so he has not moved around a lot. This may be a factor. But even if you live at a place for just a year, there's still ways to do what my grandpa did. He would always find projects to create and build in an attempt to bring designed order to the garden that was his backyard. There were paved gravel pathways, specifically chosen stones/stonework, planned out planting of trees, stone benches, and stone statues. He even had a pond put in each backyard populated with beautiful koi fish. My grandpa invests into his cosmos. He puts great attention to detail to the dressings of the world around him. This investment even carried over to the small patch of grass that is an island in their cul-de-sac. When they first moved into their current home at the end of the cul-de-sac, there was a small curbed off cement island in the middle of the road with some patchy grass on there. My grandpa eventually planted new grass, a small tree in the middle, and put a nice stone bench out under the tree just for the fun of it. This type of investment into the cosmos takes time but if you get creative, there are special ways you can start cultivating such a perspective in your life. Start with your room, or just one wall of your room. Maybe paint something yourself, and frame it. Who cares if it's good or not, most art is subjectively "good". Then hang it up somewhere. Make one corner of your house as pretty and detailed as you can. This is a start down the road of notitia, towards recognizing soul in the world around you.

In Conclusion

We set out to explore how care for the world around us, could be solidifying into what looks more like a fundamentalist religious movement that uses fire and brimstone preaching techniques to scare people into caring about the coming "apocalypse". I showed that this catastrophizing about climate change has been a rhetorical technique used for many decades to get people to care about the environment and that it's continued usage actually could do more harm than good. Despite the dangers of continually threatening people with their impending dooms, the figure heads and followers of these movements speak and act in passionate ways that sometimes breach rationalism. Instead of blaming them directly, I suggested that they might collectively be possessed by an unconscious archetype; primarily that of the great terrible Mother Earth, Gaia. It is clear from decades of depth psychology and archetypal psychology, that we as humans have dangerously neglected our own unconscious, and therefore the collective unconscious that we are all connected with. This in turn has to do with our connection to the world around us. We've neglected our own personal souls, and the soul of the world. Ancient man once had a more unconscious approach to this world and nature, and therefore found the earth around them flooded with life, teeming with gods. Ancient man found his soul in the world around him. This is something we've lost ever since our shift into modernity with the scientific revolution and the enlightenment. We then discovered that a practical approach for us to try and reconcile our loss of soul in the world would be to pay careful attention to our language and words, coupled with careful attention to the cosmos around us by making it beautiful. It is indeed our interpretation of this world around us that has everything to do with what most of the environmentalist movements claim they want to accomplish.

"This new focus would affect the ecology movement and such 'mundane matters' as energy policy, nourishment, hospital care, the design of interiors. No longer would these be external — that is, political or professional — activities only but a focus of psychotherapy, because no longer would we be able to divorce consciousness-raising of the patient from the creation itself, while illumination of the patient would be contingent upon therapy of the creation. This larger sense of therapy begins in the smaller acts of noticing." [25]

"The world's disorders are man made, enactments and projections of human subjectivity." [26]

The way to ensuring we have a future, is not by way of fear mongering. We won't get there with your radical ideas of completely rearranging the infrastructure of societal reality while destroying rights and freedoms of people all in the aim of equality. Each one of us is individually responsible. You and I are responsible for our own psyche. We have to become aware that our conscious ego is only a small part of the human mind. On top of that, we must break our gaze from constantly looking externally to outside factors. The answers lay inward. To the unconscious. The human psyche. To the soul. I think when we begin to look inward, towards all the emotions, desires, angers and resentments we've pushed deep down inside of us, then we can begin to find meaning and value in ourselves. I think when we begin to look inward by taking careful notice of our words and cosmological perspective, then we won't only find meaning and value in our lives, but find the same in this world we live in. I think once we find the soul in the world again, we can begin to move towards actually saving it, and moving towards a future for humanity before we ruin it.

Move inward to find the World Soul.

Resources

1. Jung, C., 1959. Aion. Princeton. N.J.: Princeton University Press.

2. Lomborg, Bjørn. Cool It: the Skeptical Environmentalists Guide to Global Warming. Marshall Cavendish Editions, 2010

3. Lomborg, Bjørn. Cool It: the Skeptical Environmentalists Guide to Global Warming. Marshall Cavendish Editions, 2010

4. Lomborg, Bjørn. Cool It: the Skeptical Environmentalists Guide to Global Warming. Marshall Cavendish Editions, 2010

5. Lomborg, Bjørn. Cool It: the Skeptical Environmentalists Guide to Global Warming. Marshall Cavendish Editions, 2010

6. Lomborg, Bjørn. Cool It: the Skeptical Environmentalists Guide to Global Warming. Marshall Cavendish Editions, 2010

7. Lomborg, Bjørn. Cool It: the Skeptical Environmentalists Guide to Global Warming. Marshall Cavendish Editions, 2010

8. Lomborg, Bjørn. Cool It: the Skeptical Environmentalists Guide to Global Warming. Marshall Cavendish Editions, 2010

9.   Lomborg, Bjørn. Cool It:
the Skeptical Environmentalists Guide to Global
Warming. Marshall Cavendish Editions, 2010

10.   Lomborg, Bjørn. Cool It:
the Skeptical Environmentalists Guide to Global
Warming. Marshall Cavendish Editions, 2010

11.   Lomborg, Bjørn. Cool It:
the Skeptical Environmentalists Guide to Global
Warming. Marshall Cavendish Editions, 2010

12.   Lomborg, Bjørn. Cool It:
the Skeptical Environmentalists Guide to Global
Warming. Marshall Cavendish Editions, 2010

13.   Cheetham, Tom. Imaginal Love:
the Meanings of Imagination in Henry Corbin and
James Hillman. Spring Pub., 2015.

14.   Cheetham, Tom. Imaginal Love:
the Meanings of Imagination in Henry Corbin and
James Hillman. Spring Pub., 2015.

15.   Wilber, Ken. A Brief History of Everything.
Shambhala, 2017.

16.   Wilber, Ken. A Brief History of Everything.
Shambhala, 2017.

17.   Hillman, James, and James Hillman. The Thought
of the Heart; and, the Soul of the World. Spring
Publications, 2014.

18.   Hillman, James, and James Hillman. The Thought
of the Heart; and, the Soul of the World. Spring
Publications, 2014.

19.   Hillman, James, and James Hillman. The Thought
of the Heart; and, the Soul of the World. Spring
Publications, 2014.

20.   Hillman, James, and James Hillman. The Thought
of the Heart; and, the Soul of the World. Spring
Publications, 2014.

21. Hillman, James, and James Hillman. The Thought of the Heart; and, the Soul of the World. Spring Publications, 2014.

22. Hillman, James, and James Hillman. The Thought of the Heart; and, the Soul of the World. Spring Publications, 2014.

23. Hillman, James, and James Hillman. The Thought of the Heart; and, the Soul of the World. Spring Publications, 2014.

24. Hillman, James, and James Hillman. The Thought of the Heart; and, the Soul of the World. Spring Publications, 2014.

25. Hillman, James, and James Hillman. The Thought of the Heart; and, the Soul of the World. Spring Publications, 2014.

26. Hillman, James, and James Hillman. The Thought of the Heart; and, the Soul of the World. Spring Publications, 2014.